GEOGRAPHY *for fun*

Ecosystems

Pam Robson

Franklin Watts
London • Sydney

This edition published in 2003
© Aladdin Books Ltd 2001

Produced by
Aladdin Books Ltd
28 Percy Street
London W1T 2BZ

First published in Great Britain
in 2001 by
Franklin Watts
96 Leonard Street
London EC2A 4XD

ISBN 0–7496–5354–X

Editor: Kathy Gemmell

Designer: Simon Morse

Illustrator: Tony Kenyon

Picture researcher: Brian Hunter Smart

A CIP catalogue record for this book
is available from the British Library.

The author, Pam Robson, is an experienced teacher.
She has written and advised on many books for children
on geography and science subjects.

CONTENTS

INTRODUCTION **4**

WHAT IS AN ECOSYSTEM? **6**

WHO EATS WHAT? **8**

AN OAK TREE **10**

GLOBAL ECOSYSTEMS **12**

CONIFEROUS FORESTS **14**

TROPICAL RAINFORESTS **16**

HOT DESERTS **18**

COLD DESERTS **20**

FRESHWATER ECOSYSTEMS **22**

ON THE SEASHORE **24**

SALTWATER ECOSYSTEMS **26**

WILDLIFE GARDEN **28**

ECOSYSTEMS IN DANGER **30**

GLOSSARY **31**

INDEX **32**

INTRODUCTION

Geography is about people and places and all the changes that take place in the world. What ecosystems are and how they are breaking down. How the climate affects wildlife in different parts of the world. How human progress is forcing wildlife to adapt to change. How the homes of birds and other animals are being destroyed. Geography is about all these things.

You need to know about ecosystems so that you can help wildlife survive and flourish.

1 Look out for numbers like this. Each step for the projects and surveys inside the book has been numbered in this way. Make sure you follow the steps in the right order to make the projects and complete the surveys.

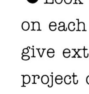

FEATURE BOXES
● Look out for the feature boxes on each double page. They either give extra information about the project on the page, or they suggest other interesting things for you to make or do.

WHAT'S HAPPENING

● The What's Happening paragraphs explain the geography behind the projects and surveys.

● Look out for Helpful Hints on some pages – they give you tips for doing the projects.

● Look up the Glossary at the back of the book to find out what important words mean.

● Always use an up-to-date atlas to find where places are.

WARNING
● This sign means that you must take care. Ask an adult first if you want to conduct a survey of a woodland, pond or seashore. Always check the times of tides if walking along a seashore. Never go out alone. Always let an adult know where you are going and what you are doing.

WHAT IS AN ECOSYSTEM?

The natural home of a plant or animal is called its habitat. Each habitat supports a different community (group) of living things. An ecosystem is made up of any given habitat and its community. The living things in an ecosystem interact with each other. They also interact with the non-living parts of their environment (surroundings), such as water or weather. Ecosystems can be large or small. A pond or even a tree is a small ecosystem. Our planet is one huge ecosystem. The study of ecosystems is called ecology.

LOCAL ECOSYSTEMS

Make a local ecosystems map.
If you can, choose an area with buildings and open spaces. You will need a large-scale map of the area, coloured pencils and a notebook.

Lichen on stones

Ants on wall

Bird's nest

Frogspawn

1 Use the large-scale map to sketch or trace an outline map of your chosen area. Draw in the roads and buildings. Ask an adult to walk round the area with you.

2 Note down or take photos of different ecosystems. There are often small ecosystems within larger ones. Look for living things interacting with non-living things, such as insects on a wall.

3 Mark on the map the locations of all the ecosystems you have observed, using different patterns or symbols for each ecosystem. Draw the symbols with pencil first, then colour them in.

4 Each ecosystem should be easy to recognise. A meadow, for example, could be shown by a tuft of grass. Design a key to explain the symbols and patterns you have used. Print names beside each one.

Building

Car park

Cemetery

Stream

Woodland and trees

Footpath

Road

Garden

Playground

Pond

Wheat field

Meadow

Hedgerow

Wall

Litter

5 Now add to your map any other details you have observed. Depending upon the season, you may have noticed a bird's nest or a fox's den. Or you may have noticed parts of an ecosystem damaged by litter pollution.

LIVING AND NON-LIVING
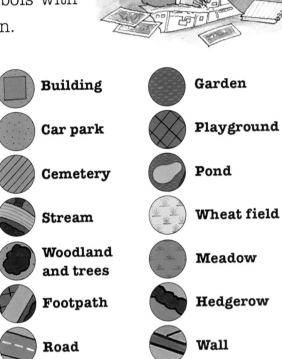
● An ecosystem is a jigsaw of living and non-living parts. The Sun and weather play a part in every ecosystem. Each part is vital. They are interdependent – if one piece is lost, the whole ecosystem breaks down. Make a list of the living and non-living parts of your ecosystems.

Ecosystem	Living parts	Non-living parts
Pond	Frogs, dragonflies, water lilies, pondweed	Water, stones, air, sunshine

WHO EATS WHAT?

All living things in an ecosystem depend upon each other for food. They are linked together in a food web. In a healthy ecosystem, there must be a balance between the number of living things that exist there. This balance is called the food pyramid. Usually, there are far fewer carnivores (meat-eaters) than herbivores (plant-eaters). The carnivores keep the number of herbivores under control. Most natural ecosystems, on land and in water, get their energy from the Sun. The Sun's energy is passed through the food pyramid.

FOOD PYRAMID

4. Large carnivores eat herbivores and small carnivores. So they are both secondary and tertiary (third-level) consumers.

3. Small carnivores eat herbivores. They are secondary (second-level) consumers.

2. Herbivores are primary (first-level) consumers. They eat green plants directly. They are prey to large and small carnivores.

1. Plants are producers – they produce their own food using energy from the Sun.

FOOD WEB

Food webs show all the members of an ecosystem community and how they interact with each other. Make your own food web to show who eats what.

Person

Bird of prey

Rabbit

Sheep

Plants

Air

Sun's energy

1 Cut out pictures of living things found in a wood. Draw and cut out a picture of the Sun, water and a cloud (for air). Glue your pictures onto folded strips of card.

2 Stand up the cards.
Use ribbon and tape to attach each animal to its food. Use red ribbon for carnivores and green ribbon for herbivores. Trace each ribbon with your finger to see how all the plants and animals are interlinked.

Fox

Bird

Mouse

Worm

Water

ENERGY FROM THE SUN

● Each chain of links in a food web, joining plants to herbivores and carnivores, is called a food chain. Most food chains start with the Sun.

● Chlorophyll, the green colour in leaves, uses the Sun's energy to make food. Sunlight turns molecules of water and a gas called carbon dioxide into sugar inside the leaf. This process is called photosynthesis.

Sugar

● In this simple food chain, a cabbage makes food using sunshine. The Sun's energy passes to the caterpillar when it eats a cabbage leaf. A bird then eats the caterpillar. When the bird dies, decomposers – small creatures and plants such as insect larvae and fungi – break down its body into the soil. This enriches the soil, which plants then use to help them grow.

Sun

Cabbage

Caterpillar

Bird

Larvae and fungi

AN OAK TREE

An oak tree supports a small ecosystem. The tree is broad-leaved and deciduous, which means it loses its leaves in winter. The oak is a rich habitat for animals and birds, which find food and building materials on and around the tree. At ground level, there are worms, insects, leaf litter, dead wood, flowers, grasses and fungi. From the ground beneath the tree to the canopy – the top of the tree – a variety of living things can be observed.

WHAT'S IN A TREE?

Make a seasonal diary for the ecosystem of an oak tree. You will need paper, an old umbrella, string, twigs and coloured pencils.

1 Hang the open umbrella from a lower branch on the tree. Shake the branch lightly. Describe or sketch any minibeasts that fall into your umbrella trap. Record your findings, then return the minibeasts to their habitat.

Spring

Date/time	Weather	
12th April 11 am	☀️☁️	
15th April 1 pm	🌧️	**Squirrel** grey
		Worm casts - lots on ground under tree
16th April 4 pm	☀️☁️	**Green woodpecker** - green body, red on head, making a drumming noise on tree trunk
18th April 10 am	☀️	**Primrose** - pale yellow flowers, 5 petals, short stems, thick dark leaves
		Wood ants - running up tree trunk

2 Ask an adult to help you press some twigs firmly into the ground around the tree. Use string to make a circle on the ground around the twigs. Write down, sketch or photograph anything you see inside the circle, such as worm casts, old acorn shells and leaves.

3 Look for small mammals and birds, such as crows, magpies or even a sparrowhawk, in the tree. Are any birds nesting? If there is a hole in the trunk, there may be a woodpecker's nest. Listen for bird songs.

Wood louse - grey; body like armour

Jay - blue, black and white feathers

Great tit

4 Write headings, for time, date and weather. Write in your observations and stick in sketches, photographs and even bark rubbings. Add labels to build up a complete picture of an oak tree ecosystem.

ON AND UNDER OAKS

● As seasons change, the oak tree menu changes for the wildlife in and around it. In autumn, large birds and mammals eat acorns. In spring, jays and magpies eat eggs stolen from nests. Blue tits eat caterpillars on leaves and buds.

● Nature recycles its waste. Under a tree, you will find decomposers that feed and grow on dead plants and animals, breaking them down into the soil (see below). Decomposed matter does not hold energy, but provides the soil with nutrients (goodness).

Fungi grow on dead logs and leaves.

Ants, beetles and other small creatures eat droppings and fungi.

Bacteria break down anything that remains.

GLOBAL ECOSYSTEMS

The world is split into large ecosystems called biomes. Biomes are named after the main type of vegetation (plant life) that grows there. They are shaped by climate – how hot, cold, wet or dry a place is. Tropical forests have lots of rain and sunshine. Deserts are hot and dry. The tundra (cold desert) is freezing. Mountain tops are also cold. Temperate areas have a warm, moist climate and are rarely very hot or very cold. Each place has its own food web, with wildlife that has adapted to the climate there.

Tundra
Coniferous forest
Temperate grasslands
Temperate forest
Mountains
Desert
Scrub
Savanna
Seasonal tropical forest
Tropical rainforest

Climate depends upon latitude (how far north or south of the Equator a place is) and altitude (height above sea level).

Ice
Tundra
Coniferous forest
Temperate grasslands
Temperate forest
Scrub
Mountains
Desert
Savanna
Seasonal tropical forest
Tropical rainforest

Equator

Biomes of the world

ISLANDS

● Islands often have unique ecosystems. The Galapagos Islands, off the coast of Ecuador, are home to some of the world's rarest creatures, such as giant tortoises and sea lizards (right).

BIOME CARD GAME

To make this game, you will need stiff card, scissors and coloured pencils. Each set of cards shows a food chain in a different biome.

1 Cut out 30 pieces of card. Copy the pictures on the cards shown here, until you have two sets of each food chain and six Sun cards. Number and label each set, as shown.

Sun (all sets)

x 6

Temperate forest set

x 2

Tropical rainforest set

x 2

Tundra set

x 2

Desert set

x 2

2 Two or more can play. The aim is to collect four cards belonging to the same set. All sets must include a Sun card (1). Each player begins with four cards. Take turns to pick a card from the pile. Either keep that card or replace it at the bottom of the pile. The first person to collect a whole food chain is the winner.

ADDING MORE CARDS
● Find out about more food chains, in these or other biomes, and make cards for them. Make sure you always have a plant, a herbivore and a carnivore. Make up a symbol for each new biome.

CONIFEROUS FORESTS

Coniferous trees are softwoods. They have needle-like leaves that stay green throughout the year. They grow best in cold climates and on mountain sides. In coniferous forests, sunshine rarely reaches the forest floor. This means that the ecosystems in coniferous forests are not as rich as in broad-leaved forests, because few plants grow with so little light. The diversity (variety) of wildlife is not as great, as there are fewer plants for animals and birds to eat. There are not many natural coniferous forests left today – most are now planted by foresters.

Dry

Crossbills use their special beak to extract seeds from inside pine cones.

Most conifers are pines, firs or spruces.

Few plants grow on the dark forest floor.

Chipmunks hibernate in winter.

Canadian coniferous forest
1. Crossbill
2. Douglas fir
3. Canada geese
4. Owl
5. Spruce
6. Lynx
7. Moose
8. Chipmunk
9. Weevil

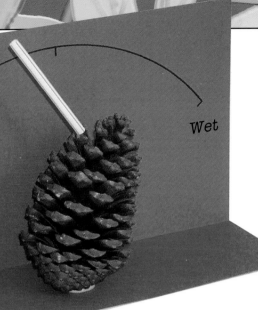

Wet

CONE GAUGE

Use a pine cone to make a hygrometer. This measures humidity – moisture in the air. You will need a pine cone, a headed pin, a plastic drinking straw, a sheet of card, plasticine and a pen.

1 Stick the headed pin into one of the middle scales of the cone. Push a straw over the end of the pin.

2 Fold the card and draw a scale on it, as shown below. Position the cone on the card using plasticine, as shown above. Place it outside, sheltered from rain. Wait and see which way the straw moves in moist air. Now label the scale 'wet' at one end and 'dry' at the other.

WHAT'S HAPPENING

● Pine cones hold the seeds of conifers. They close when the air is moist and it is about to rain, to protect the seeds inside. The outside scales absorb the moisture in the air, swell up and bend inwards to close.

Seed

SUSTAINABLE FORESTRY

● In many parts of the world, the wildlife-rich natural vegetation has been cut down and replaced by coniferous plantations. The conifers are then cut down to make paper and furniture. Now foresters practise sustainable forestry. This means they cut down only part of the coniferous plantation at a time so that ecosystems can survive.

TROPICAL RAINFORESTS

Many of the world's plant and animal species live in tropical rainforests, where the climate is always warm and moist. The Amazon rainforest in South America is like a huge block of flats, with different living things at each level. At the bottom is the dark forest floor, then the herb layer, shrub layer, understorey, canopy and, at the top, the emergent layer. Hardwood trees grow tall and straight as they struggle to reach the Sun. They are so tall that they have roots above the ground, called buttress roots.

Emergent layer – the tallest trees push through the canopy to reach the Sun.

Understorey – younger trees strive to reach the sunlight.

Herb layer – ferns and herbs grow. Tapirs and insects live here.

Canopy – treetops are bound together by creepers and climbing plants. Home to orchids, birds, monkeys, snakes and lizards.

Shrub layer – young trees grow from seedlings. Woody plants with large leaves and colourful flowers grow here.

Forest floor – rotting leaf litter covers the poor soil. Few plants grow here, except along rivers, where some sunshine gets through.

MINI RAINFOREST

To create a mini rainforest, you will need a small fishtank with a lid (or cling film), compost, charcoal, gravel and suitable plants, such as ferns, mosses, orchids and African violets.

1 Line the bottom of the tank with a layer of charcoal and gravel. Cover with a layer of compost. Make the soil damp before arranging your plants.

2 Arrange the plants before planting. Do not put them too close together as they will need room to grow.

3 Place the lid (or cling film) over the tank and put in a warm spot, but not in direct sunlight. Water every few weeks. The lid will keep the soil moist.

WHAT'S HAPPENING

● Rainforests play a big part in controlling the world's climate. Without trees, there would be less rainfall. Leaves transpire, which means they lose water through tiny holes. Transpiration helps make the air moist. The leaves on the plants in your tank will transpire and keep the air and soil moist.

● Thunderstorms are frequent in rainforests as the warm, moist air rises quickly and cools.

Fast-rising moist air condenses into droplets, which form high thunderclouds.

Cool air

Moist air, including transpiration

Warm air

Heavy rain

Soil is kept moist

EPIPHYTES
● Epiphytes are rainforest plants that grow on other plants. Some grow in the low, darker parts of the forest. Others, like orchids, like the sunshine of the canopy.

DEFORESTATION
● Half the world's rainforests have been destroyed. Some people cut down trees to farm the land for food. Others cut down trees to sell the timber.

HOT DESERTS

Living things struggle to survive in hot, dry deserts. Many have learned some very strange habits, just to stay alive. The spade-foot toad, found in the Sonoran Desert of Arizona, hibernates underground for most of the year. When the annual midsummer rain approaches, it emerges to mate and lay its eggs in pools of rainwater. Within days, the eggs hatch and become tadpoles, then toads. Then the toads disappear underground again. Desert plants have to survive for long periods without rain. Many survive as seeds. Cacti have shallow roots, close to the surface, ready to catch any rain that falls.

PLANT A DESERT GARDEN

To create a desert garden, you will need a shallow clay bowl, sand and compost, pebbles or gravel, protective gloves and some small cactus plants, such as bunny ears, peanut cactus, golden barrel cactus and hedge cactus. Ask at your local garden centre for advice on which cacti to buy.

1 Mix together the sand and compost. Fill the bowl three-quarters full with the soil mixture.

2 Put on protective gloves, then plant your cacti. After planting, cover the surface of the soil with pebbles or gravel.

Gila monster

DESERT ANIMALS AND PEOPLES

● Desert animals have had to adapt to hot, dry conditions. In North America, a poisonous lizard called the Gila monster stores fat in its thick tail. It can live on this fat for months without eating. Birds called roadrunners save energy by running instead of flying. Ground squirrels in the Kalahari Desert in southern Africa use their plumed tails as sunshades.

● For thousands of years, the only people living in the Great Australian Desert were Aboriginal nomads – people who regularly move from place to place. Now, most Australian Aborigines live in towns and cities. Bedouins have lived in the deserts of North Africa and Syria for centuries. A few still live as nomads, travelling from oasis to oasis.

Bedouins

HELPFUL HINTS

● Place your desert garden in a sunny position.
● Cacti have sharp spikes, so handle them with care. Use thick leather or suede gloves to protect your hands when handling cacti.
● Do not water your garden too often. Cacti need only a small amount of water. Too much water will cause the stems to rot and will leave a black mark.

COLD DESERTS

Cold deserts, called tundra, are places where the ground is frozen for much of the year. Alpine tundra is found at high altitudes, above the tree line. In the Arctic, there are no trees, only grasses, mosses and lichens. Lichens are fungi that contain algae. They appear as crusty patches or shrubby growths on rocks. Shrubby lichens can only survive in clean air. They are an important part of tundra ecosystems, and are threatened by pollution, which can be carried a great distance by winds and water.

North of the tundra is the Arctic icecap.

Below the surface is permafrost, which is ground that is frozen all year round.

The tundra has rocky mounds called pingoes and long lakes.

Below the tundra is a belt of coniferous forest, called the taiga.

LOOKING FOR LICHENS

One way to check pollution in your area is to look for lichens. The nature and colour of any lichens will indicate air quality. If you find only green algae, the air is probably heavily polluted.

1 Ask an adult to come with you to look at local lichens. Look on walls, stones, trees and gravestones. Record the colour and location of any lichens you see. Sketch their appearance. Check the scale opposite to help you identify the lichens.

2 Mark your lichen findings on the ecosystems map you made on page 6. Make up a key to show the type of lichen found. Write in the date on which you found them.

Polluted

GREEN ALGAE
Found in heavily polluted areas. Probably no lichens.

GREY-GREEN CRUSTY LICHENS
Often found on gravestones. High-level air pollution.

ORANGE CRUSTY LICHENS
Also found on gravestones. Medium-level air pollution

LEAFY LICHENS
Found on walls and trees. Low-level air pollution.

SHRUBBY LICHENS
Found on rocks and trees. Clean air.

Clean

Lichens can live for 4,000 years. They can survive all climatic conditions. There are 25,000 known species. They grow slowly, only 1 cm each year.

SYMBIOSIS AND CAMOUFLAGE

● Symbiosis is a partnership between two living things, from which both benefit. The fungi and algae that make up lichens are symbiotic. The fungi absorb water and minerals, then the algae use these to turn

sunshine into food by photosynthesis (see page 9). Both the fungi and algae gain from living together.
● Camouflage is the ability of certain animals to blend in with their natural surroundings and so hide from predators. But predators also use camouflage to hide from their prey.

Arctic fox in summer

Arctic fox in winter

21

FRESHWATER ECOSYSTEMS

In ponds and lakes, where the water is still, plant life is rich. Rivers and streams have running water, so there is less plant life.

Large predators like perch eat smaller fish. Too many predators in a pond destroy the ecosystem because the secondary consumers are all eaten up. Without secondary consumers to control numbers, the primary consumers increase and eat all the plant life. Without plant life, the pond ecosystem breaks down completely.

ZONE 3: DEEP WATER

ZONE 2: SHALLOW WATER OR SWAMP

Great reedmace

Arrowhead

Water lily

Water crowfoot

Milfoil

POND ZONES

Pond animals move around, but plants remain in one place. Make a pond chart, dividing it into zones according to the plants found there. Take care near water. Always tell an adult what you are doing.

1 Make sketches and take notes about the plants in and around the pond. Look first at the bank, then at the shallow water, or swampy area around the edge, then at the deep water. Here, you will only be able to see the tops of the plants. Some plants live completely beneath the water.

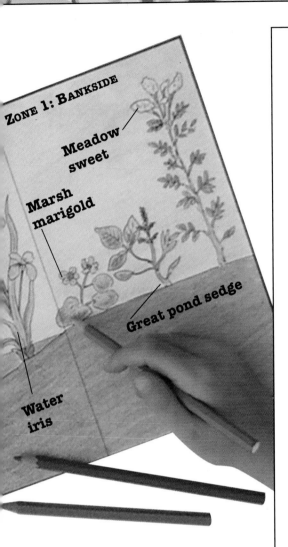

ZONE 1: BANKSIDE

Meadow sweet

Marsh marigold

Great pond sedge

Water iris

POND LIFE

● Birds that live and feed near fresh water have adapted special feet and beaks. The heron has a long, thin beak with which to catch fish or frogs. It has long legs so that it can stand for a long time in deep water waiting for prey.

Flamingo

Avocet

Heron

● Everything in a pond food web depends on plant life, even if you cannot see any plants. Big fish eat small fish, which eat dragonfly larvae, which eat tiny creatures, which feed on microscopic plants.

Dragonfly

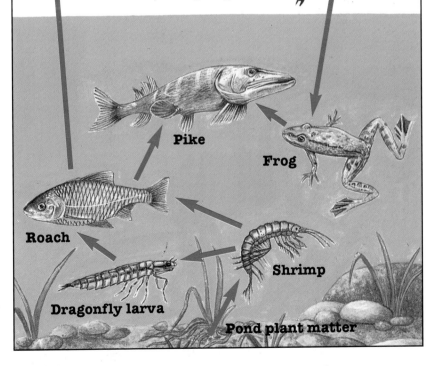

Pike

Frog

Roach

Dragonfly larva

Shrimp

Pond plant matter

2 Sketch a cross section of the pond and divide it into zones, as shown here. Zone 1 is the bankside, Zone 2 is the shallow water or swamp area and Zone 3 is the deep water. Underwater plants, called submerged aquatics, go in the deep water zone. Fill in details about each plant. Use a field guide to help you identify any plants not shown here.

ON THE SEASHORE

There are sandy, shingle and rocky beaches. Each provides a different habitat, but all are affected by the same tidal movements. There are two high and two low tides every day. Very high tides, called spring tides, happen twice a month. Between high-water spring tide marks and low-water spring tide marks, there are five seashore zones. In these zones, plants and animals have adapted to produce a variety of ecosystems. Different seaweeds and shells are found in each zone.

BEACHCOMBER

Next time you go to a beach, carry out a beach ecosystem survey. Tell an adult where you are going and ask a friend to come with you. Always check the times of high tides. Carry out your study at low tide. Select a quiet stretch of beach to study.

Splash zone

Upper shore

High tide mark

Middle shore

Lower shore

1 Stretch a length of string from the top of the beach to the edge of the water. Hold each end in place with a pebble. Mark the string with a pen where you think each zone ends. The five zones are lower shore, middle shore, upper shore, high tide mark and splash zone.

2 List the differences you notice between the zones. Collect shells, pebbles and small pieces of seaweed and driftwood. Note carefully which zone you found them in. Record the date, time and weather conditions.

JETSAM
● Storms at sea often carry jetsam (rubbish from ships) onto beaches. Ropes, bottles and tins are found amongst

seaweed and shells after bad weather. Containers holding dangerous chemicals have been found on beaches. These can gradually alter ecosystems.

SAND DUNES
● Grasses have long roots that hold the sand down in ridges. This prevents the sand from blowing away. Marram grass is often planted in sand dunes to stop the sand blowing any further.

ROCK POOLS
● Rock pools are left behind when the tide goes out. Plants and animals that live in rock pools cannot survive out of water. In rock pools, you can find sea anemones, crabs, sea urchins, starfish, seaweeds, shrimps and prawns. Small fish like blennies and gobies are also found in pools. Always replace any rocks that you move.

3 Map the area of beach you have surveyed on a large sheet of card. Draw in the zones created by high- and low-water marks. Glue on and label everything you have collected.

Rock pool

SALTWATER ECOSYSTEMS

The ocean is the largest habitat on Earth. But sea animals depend upon plants for their food, just as land animals do. The most important marine plants, called phytoplankton, are so small that they can only be seen with a microscope. Phytoplankton are the primary producers in the food chains of the sea. They grow near the surface, where sunlight causes photosynthesis to happen. Microscopic animals called zooplankton then feed on phytoplankton, and larger animals eat the zooplankton.

Killer whale

Tern

Seal

Squid

Fish

Krill

OCEAN FOOD WEB

Phytoplankton are single-celled algae. If you get a chance, look at a sample of sea water under a microscope, and you will see the pretty patterns on phytoplankton.

Zooplankton

Phytoplankton

SALTY FACTS

● A food web of the sea includes some of the smallest and largest living things in the world – the blue whale and krill. Krill are tiny shrimp-like forms of zooplankton, found in the seas of the Antarctic. Amazingly, they are the only food the blue whale eats. The blue whale can be up to 30 m long. It strains the krill from the sea through the baleen inside its mouth, which acts like a sieve.

Blue whale

Krill

1. Corals grow around a volcanic island.

2. The volcano erodes and a lagoon forms.

3. The volcano sinks completely. The reef remains with small, sandy islands on top.

● In tropical seas, there are low islands called coral reefs that are formed by tiny creatures called polyps. The jelly-like polyps build up hard skeletons of calcium carbonate. When they die, the skeletons are left as coral. New polyps grow on top of the dead ones. Coral needs warmth and light, so it grows only near the ocean's surface.

● Coastal mangrove swamp forests are types of tropical forest. Mangrove trees have adapted to survive in the salty water in mud estuaries of tropical rivers. They have special roots that keep the leaves above the water and allow the plant to obtain more oxygen. Mangroves are the habitat of many species, such as fiddler crabs, and are breeding grounds for reef fish.

WILDLIFE GARDEN

As your contribution towards preserving healthy ecosystems, you could make a wildlife garden. Even if you do not have your own garden, you can encourage wildlife by cultivating plants in a window box or on a balcony. Plant flowers with strong colours and scents that will attract insects such as bees and butterflies. Peacock butterflies like to lay their eggs beneath nettle leaves. These pages will give you some ideas on how to create a wildlife garden.

A SPACE FOR WILDLIFE

Diversity is the key to a successful wildlife garden. Diversity means providing many different habitats – shady areas, sunny spots and open spaces. This will attract many creatures. You could make a habitat pile, from logs, to attract insects. Make a bird table so that birds can feed safely. You could even build a pond.

HELPFUL HINTS

● Choose the east- or west-facing side of a tree trunk for a bird box. A south-facing nest may harm fledglings because they will become too warm.

● A log pile will encourage minibeasts into your wildlife garden. It will also encourage small birds like robins which feed on insects.

● Leave an area of garden with long grass – this will also encourage minibeasts.

BIRD FEEDER

Make environmentally friendly pine cone bird feeders. You need some long pine cones, a ball of string, a spoon, unsweetened peanut butter, bird seed, greaseproof paper and a baking tray.

1 First, cut a length of string for each pine cone. Loop and tie the string to one end of each cone.

2 Use a spoon to smear peanut butter all over each pine cone. Make sure it covers every part of the cone. Press firmly into all the spaces.

3 Sprinkle bird seed onto the greaseproof paper on the baking tray. Roll the cones in the bird seed until they are all well covered. The bird seed will stick to the peanut butter. Shake off any loose seed.

4 Birds like to feed where they are safe from predators like cats. Position your pine cone bird feeders away from shrubbery, trees and fences. A tree stump or bird table in the centre of an open space is a safe site.

CONTRACT WITH NATURE

● As houses and roads are built, animals and plants are losing their natural habitats. Even common birds like sparrows are disappearing. Remind yourself to do what you can to encourage wildlife by making a contract with nature.

Contract with nature

I ....

Promise ....

Signed ....

ECOSYSTEMS IN DANGER

The habitats and the wildlife that together make up ecosystems are in danger. Tropical rainforests are especially rich in animal and plant life. It is thought that they contain between 60% and 80% of all the land species on Earth. Some species there are now threatened with extinction.

Rainforest destruction

● An area of rainforest the size of 37 football pitches is lost every minute, to provide wood or farmland.

● The tiny golden lion tamarin of Brazil's Atlantic coastal rainforest is threatened by the loss of its habitat. Today, there are only about 700 left.

About 90% of Brazil's Atlantic coastal rainforest has now been destroyed.

S. America

Golden lion tamarin

● A parrot called the Spix's macaw also lives in the Brazilian rainforest. Although there are a few captive birds, there is now thought to be only a single wild one left.

● One fifth of the world's tropical forests are found in Africa. In the Congo Basin, 4 million hectares of forest are destroyed each year to clear the ground for farming. In 1999, five central African countries signed the Yaounde Declaration, an agreement to save huge areas of forest in the Congo Basin.

Amazing survivors

● The Australian thorny devil can survive in its desert environment without drinking. It gets moisture from the black ants on which it feeds. Grooves on its skin channel moisture from dew into the corners of its mouth.

● The eggs of the fairy shrimp can survive for 10,000 years until water activates them.

● The hawkmoth caterpillar has a clever disguise – the patterns on its body make it look just like a snake!

● A chameleon catches its fast-moving insect prey with its tongue, which can move much faster than its body.

GLOSSARY

Bacteria (sing. **bacterium**)
Single-celled organisms
(living things) found in
soil that help break
down dead matter.

Biome
A large ecosystem,
usually named after the
type of vegetation that
grows there.

Camouflage
The use of colour or
pattern that enables an
animal or plant to merge
with its surroundings.

Carnivore
A meat-eater.

Climate
The average weather in
a place over the year.

Community
The plants and animals
within one habitat.

Consumer
An animal or plant that
eats other living things.

Decomposer
An organism that breaks
down dead plant and
animal matter, releasing
minerals into the soil.

Ecology
The study of ecosystems.

Ecosystem
One community in one
habitat and its non-living
environment.

Environment
The surroundings of a
habitat.

Epiphyte
A plant that grows on
another plant without
feeding from it.

Habitat
The natural home of a
plant or animal.

Herbivore
A plant-eater.

Hibernation
Long sleep taken by some
animals to save energy
when food is scarce.

Lichen
An organism composed
of two living things,
algae and fungi.

Photosynthesis
The process that plants
use to make food, using
sunlight and chlorophyll
(the green colour
in plants).

Phytoplankton
Microscopic plant life
found on the surface
of oceans.

Predator
An animal that hunts
and eats other animals.

Prey
An animal hunted and
eaten by a predator.

Producer
A green plant that
makes food through
photosynthesis.

Symbiosis
A partnership that
benefits two different
species.

Vegetation
Plant life, especially
of a particular region.

Zooplankton
Microscopic marine
animal life that feeds
on phytoplankton.

INDEX

algae 20, 21, 26, 31

bacteria 11, 31
biomes 12, 13, 31
birds 4, 6, 7, 9, 10, 11, 14, 16, 19, 23, 28, 29

camouflage 21, 31
carnivores 8, 9, 13, 31
chlorophyll 9, 31
climate 4, 12, 14, 16, 17, 21, 31
communities 6, 8, 31
coniferous forests 12, 14, 15, 20
consumers 8, 22, 31
coral reefs 27

decomposers 9, 11, 31
deforestation 17, 30
deserts 12, 13, 18, 19, 20, 30

ecology 6, 31
environment 6, 30, 31
epiphytes 17, 31

food chains 9, 12, 13, 26
food pyramids 8
food webs 8, 9, 12, 23, 27
fungi 9, 10, 11, 20, 21, 31

habitats 6, 10, 24, 26, 27, 28, 29, 30, 31
herbivores 8, 9, 13, 31
hibernation 14, 18, 31

insects 6, 9, 10, 16, 28, 30

islands 12

lichens 6, 13, 20, 21, 31

mangroves 27
minibeasts 10, 28
mountains 12, 14

photosynthesis 9, 21, 26, 31
phytoplankton 26, 31
pollution 7, 20, 21

ponds 5, 6, 7, 22, 23, 28
predators 21, 22, 29, 31
prey 8, 21, 23, 30, 31
producers 8, 26, 31

rainforests 12, 13, 16, 17, 30
rock pools 25

savanna 12
scrub 12
seashores 5, 24
Sun, the 7, 8, 9, 13, 16
sustainable forestry 15
symbiosis 21, 31

temperate areas 12, 13
thunderstorms 17
tides 5, 24, 25
transpiration 17
trees 6, 10, 11, 14, 16, 17, 20, 21, 27, 29
tundra 12, 13, 20

vegetation 12, 15, 31

zooplankton 26, 27, 31

PICTURE CREDITS
Abbreviations: t-top, m-middle, b-bottom, r-right, l-left, c-centre.
All photographs supplied by Select Pictures except for: 5tl, 10ml, 17br –
Digital Stock. 15bl – Rolf Bender/FLPA–Images of Nature. 18ml – Jurgen
& Christine Sohns/FLPA–Images of Nature. 20c – G T Andrewartha/FLPA
–Images of Nature. 22ml – Ian Rose/FLPA–Images of Nature. 25tr – David
Hosking/FLPA–Images of Nature. 26ml – Corbis. 27mr – Stockbyte.